POEMS

of

SORTS 2+

POEMS

of

SORTS 2+

Bob Rutzel

1603 Capitol Ave., Suite 310 Cheyenne, Wyoming USA 82001
1-888-980-6523 | admin@urlinkpublishing.com

URLink Print and Media is committed to excellence in the publishing industry.

Published in the United States of America

ISBN 978-1-64367-626-5 (Paperback)
ISBN 978-1-64367-625-8 (Digital)

03.07.19

ACKNOWLEDGEMENTS

My first book (Poems of Sorts) dealt with thoughts we all have had in Poem format. Some rhymed, most did not because rhyming is hard and I believed - still do – that the thoughts were what counted most. Plus the poem format is easier to see the beginning, middle and ending. But all poems should be spoken aloud as they are easier to understand when spoken.

Many of the poems or thoughts In Poems of Sorts were actually true stories that had some humor in them. Yes, many were completely made up. You should be able to tell. It's called being creative.

The same people who encouraged me the most remain: the late Ron Barry (English Teacher in Syosset High); Niece Krystyn (Rutzel) Serrano; Annita-Tex (Harless) Sours; John Delin, my Captain from the Safety Patrol back in the day; and the late Bob Thomas writer of Golf Book Stories who was a wealth of knowledge regarding writing books; and also Kat DeMille, who gave insightful reviews on the draft of Poems of Sorts and in here too.

After Poems of Sorts I had newer encouragements: my aunt Doris Rogalski; my brother Larry Rutzel; and good friend Marilyn Soloman; and Mary Joan Corcoran, who is always supportive and gives good advice; and Dave Schartung who made several suggestions that were taken. All have asked when the next book was coming out as they really enjoyed Poems of Sorts.

Anyway thank you one and all.

MY POEMS PLUS

The poems or thoughts that either rhyme or not kept coming and it was time to do another book. My family jumped up and down when I told them another book was coming out. Now it's time for the rest of you to jump up and down, too. Well, let's hope.

The poem format is still used because it is easier to see the beginning, middle and ending of a thought and usually it's on one page. And, above all poems that rhyme or not should be read aloud as that way they are easier to understand. Try it. You'll see. Sometimes in rhyming, one loses the thought by concentrating on the last word in a sentence trying to figure out what word would be used to help the rhyme in the next sentence. See? Doing non-rhyme My way you do not lose the thought - and truth be told - it may be a thought you have always had and it may be an important one.

Again, I have tried to stay faithful to Samuel Taylor Coleridge's words "poetry is the best words in the best order."

Next up is Albert Finch and you will come to know he is your best advisor in all things. And you never knew he was available and cheap too.

The In The Grave Section gives some insight to those departed, but who live on in another way. And who is to say all this is not true. One day we may all find out for sure. Let's hope.

The question was asked to whom is the person in the grave talking to. He is talking to the person who is reading the In The Grave section.

ALBERT FINCH

ALBERT FINCH

You may have never heard of Albert Finch, but he knows all about you. You may have never seen Albert Finch, but he sees you all the time. He sees what you do and what you do not do. No, he is not God, the Tooth Fairy, or your Guardian Angel, but he watches us all hoping we all do the right thing when the time comes. And when does that time come? Actually, all the time, every second of every day, day in and day out.

Only a few people on this Earth have had actual contact with Albert Finch and - truth be told - they are far better for it and they come to know exactly who he is, but many do not. You may think he may be very old for this to happen to the many, many he has contacted over the many, many years, but think thousands of years and you may be almost close. Almost close. Almost.

Where exactly is Albert Finch? No one really knows. He may be the auto mechanic you need to get your car going, he could be the runner you just passed thinking he needs to fun faster, he may be the waitress who served you breakfast, he may be a distant family member you never knew you had until now. You balked when I said "waitress" and I should tell you that Albert Finch is not some kind of Shape-Shifter. No he is more than that. One never knows how or when Albert Finch will show up, but he comes when he is needed regardless of your station in life. The sad part of this is that most do not know they are being contacted or helped by Albert Finch. Very sad. And it is here that the wrong decisions are made and this makes Albert Finch sad, sad, very sad.

Now you may think I am making all this up. No. Albert Finch is very real, ageless and always on the job and has been around for thousands of years always trying to get us to do the right thing.

Albert Finch is known by many names, but I came to know him as Albert Finch. Kind of catchy, don't you think? Well, Albert Finch thought so too. His only regret is that others know him by other names. You see, he likes the name Albert Finch a lot. Where the name came from even Albert Finch does not know, and he doesn't dwell on it as he has only one purpose and that is to make sure we are helped in the best way possible.

Again, Albert Finch is not God, the Tooth Fairy, or your Guardian Angel. Please stop comparing him to them. I know it's tempting and may be close, but not true.

The last time I was in contact with Albert Finch I learned what he had been up to and he seemed kind of proud about it. I learned he helped little Johnny K. apologize to his father for talking back to him; 8-year old Marie made a good decision to talk to her mother about a boy in her class who kept looking at her; and Tim paid back the money he owed Thomas W. going on 10-years and now they talk regularly. Albert Finch said there is still much to do.

I asked Albert Finch if he had any success with world leaders who seemed not to abide by the rules of a civilized society. Sadly, Albert Finch says he had done all he could, but did not have any success. However, it is not in Albert Finch's make-up to quit and he will, of course, keep trying. And for that we are grateful. Very grateful.

Leaving world problems aside, I had a problem and Albert Finch is taking his time getting back to me, but I trust him and will wait as this is not an easy problem with solution.

Finally, Albert Finch said to stay away and not go there as going there will create more problems that I do not need; say nothing, do nothing. Hmmmm........... Well, okay. Guess that is that. Okay. Okay.

However, Albert Finch did say that there is another Player in play and this Player will overrule him at times, and Albert Finch is okay with that. But this time Albert Finch and this other Player are in total agreement.

I wanted to know who this Player is and Albert Finch says it is the person - and he did use these exact words - "or Entity" who keeps people on the straight and narrow. Who is this person or Entity I wanted to know. Albert Finch says no one knows for sure who this Player is as he never seen, but is always around. Much like you I asked. Not at all this time Albert Finch says.

I thank Albert Finch for his advice and will, of course, take it. So it looks like Albert Finch and this other Player are teaming up to keep me on level ground, and that is a good thing. For sure. For sure.

Okay, you just saw an incident whereby I talked to and received advice from Albert Finch and may be wondering if you could do the same and be helped by him. Yes, of course, you can. It will happen without a doubt when you look deep inside yourself and Albert Finch will appear. You may call him something else, but remember: he likes the name Albert Finch.

POEMS OF SORTS

MY WEED-WHACKER

Clare, a teenage girl, weed-whacks the weeds by
my fences, the out buildings, the house and garage.
The problem is I will lose her soon as she will go to college;
But that's not the worst part.
She has a singing talent and has an incredible
natural Country-Western quality to her voice, and
she doesn't use a guitar when she sings.
What a disaster for me.
Now what do I do? What do I do?
How will my weeds get whacked
to make the fences, out-buildings, house and garage
look so manicured?
How indeed?
What to do? What to do?
I took some time to assess the situation
and made a decision:
I told Clare to get a guitar.

A CHRISTMAS SONG

Haven't they all been done?
Christmas is all about a feeling
of a birth, and joy and tears welling
so eyes cannot see clearly,
but look
with a clear memory of how it was
that first Day.
How to start?
On that day of days
calendars were re-written
as a new history began ……….
And so it was and is for all time
that Joy came into the world
and has never left us
and this song will never be done.

A RESUME VS A POEM

A resume is like a poem in that
there is always something that can
be taken out or put in.
The objective of a resume is to
get one to the interview.
The objective of a poem ....
Hmmmmm............
Well, there are many, many
objectives....................

A SIGMOIDOSCOPY

How lucky many are today when
they need a colon exam.
But not me back in the day.
When in the USAF I had
pains on my right side no one could explain.
I was to be given a sigmoidoscopy.
Naked on a 3-step stool with butt pointed
at the ceiling, a silver pipe of sorts was
inserted with probes and a light to check for
cancer and anything else.
What a trying uncomfortable time.
All was good, but the Major said he
needed to do it again and have another doctor
witness. I pleaded not to have it again.
No luck. We did it again.
Did I mention how uncomfortable this was?
Still all was good again, thank goodness.
Today the patient lies on his side on soft
mattress, a little anesthesia and lights out.
Will hardly know anything was happening.
How lucky many are today.......................
The pain? It was decided I ate too many greasy
foods at the airport cafeteria.

A SORT OF MIRACLE

Consider this: you are in the 7th and 8th
grades and play baseball against the
other schools in the area and every one
of those schools have really good players.
Sometime they win and if you win it was
a really tough game.
Then a miracle happens.
You all go to the same High School
and you are all on the same team.
How good is that?
And now there is a feeling that
no one can beat us.
That happened.

A WOMAN'S PLEASANT VOICE

I had a late night last night
and I laid there in the bed in the morning
and enjoyed the warmth with the cold wind
howling outside.
Then I heard a soft woman's voice
that said: Ohoooooo.
I have no idea who that was, but I
had to laugh to myself as that
was a very pleasant voice.
Maybe I should have stayed there and
possibly heard more, but I got up.
My friend said he bought copper dowsing rods
to contact spirits as that is possible, he says.
Do I want to do that?
No, instead
I will wait next time for that voice to say
more.

ANSWERS

We have been told that all answers to
the mysteries in life
will be told to us upon our deaths.
Hey, I do not want to wait until then.
I want to know now.
However all we can do - and we do this -
is to come up with various theories,
and wonder if we are getting it right or
just coming close....... or not.

BE BACK

She said she'd come right back.
Haven't seen her since that time
long ago.
Of course, I still wait.
One never knows.
Could happen………………..

BIGGEST REGRET

If I ever win a lottery
I have my eye on 9-cars
and a Pick-up Truck.
My biggest regret
would be
that I wouldn't be able
to drive all 10 at the
same time.

BLAME

Q: Were you ever bullied?

M: No.

Q: Were you ever a bully?

M: No.

Q: Were you ever arrested?

M: No.

Q: Were you ever disrespectful to your parents?

M: No.

Q: Did you ever cheat in school?

M: No.

Q: Did you ever steal anything?

M: No.

Q: Did you ever start a fight?

M: No.

Q: Did you ever lie about anything important?

M: No.

Q: Were you ever mean to anyone?

M: No.

Q: This is hard to believe. How do you account for all this?

M: I blame it on my parents.

BRAIN FREEZE

Why can't we get our brain to do
simple things?
Like having the brain take care
of that itch?
Keeping our feet warm.
No, the brain only operates on
external things.
For everything internal, the brain
forces us to move the hand to
scratch the itch, or
go find blankets or warmer socks.
Okay, we get it, but
Lottery numbers are
External things.......oh, we get
numbers
Just never the right ones, and
we still call the brain, a brain?
Go figure.

CAR SEATS

In 1965, I had the opportunity to sit
in a Rolls Royce.
Have no idea what year it was, but
I can still feel the comfort of the seat
to this day.
All this tells me the car makers can sell
more of their cars a lot quicker
if they made the front seats more comfortable.
They don't listen.
Today, those seats are hard and
not comfortable at all.
These car makers should take a lesson
from Rolls Royce makers.
And, of course, I am available for a
Finders Fee. Ha!

CAREFUL

As we get older I must tell you
to be very careful as you go
as there may be things in your way
that you don't see or think you
can navigate easily.
You cannot as you are no longer young
as you once were.
There will be times you will hurt
yourself.
How do I know?
I know.
I have bruises.

COMFORT ZONE

A while back, the son asked the mother
about his brother who passed,
"Do you ever think of Gary?"
"All the time", she replied.
"I think about him working on his house
In New Orleans and getting permissions
to do this and that. It's easier to think of him
in that way. I know he's gone, but this way it's kind of comforting."
The son now thinks about his mother who passed
In almost the same way as he remembers her
going about household chores, talking to friends
on the telephone and so on.
Both brother and mother are now gone,
But the son keeps them alive in this
comfort zone.

CONTESTS

I enter many contests
for money.
Do I ever win?
Of course not.
Why not?
I think it is because there was never
any intention to give out the money
and believe it's all a scam
Why do I keep entering these contests?
Why indeed?
I could be wrong.

CROSSROADS

Let's face it
We live in Crossroads 24/7.
How so?
There are choices we must make
every day:
Left or right?
Up or down?
Yes or no?
This way or that way?
Go or not go?
Stay or not stay?
Do this or that?
See?
We need to make one choice
not caring what would have
happened had we made the other.
See?

DEATH RAY BUTTON

I used to have that button
on my car dash.
Sold the car, forgot to take
the button.
Now when someone annoys
me, I wish them a flat tire, sometimes
two, but
still wish I had that Death Ray Button
back....................
Still looking for it.

DIFFERENT REFLECTIONS

A Cardinal bird attacks the outside mirror on
my pick-up and does so regularly.
I think it sees another bird who is encroaching on
his territory and wants it gone.
But don't we do the same thing when we look
into a mirror?
We see things that we want gone or manicured a bit
to make us more acceptable to the world, and okay,
to ourselves?
And when we do this, aren't we trying to look like a
work of art along with our clothes? Of course.
But the main thrust is to make sure we get gone
those things that need to be gone or trimmed up.
We can do this.
But that bird can't.
It just wants that other bird gone.

DIRECTIONS

I am the worst one to follow
someone's directions to me to
go somewhere.
They always leave something out,
something I really needed.
The problem is that they assume
too much about what I know.
How wrong.
Why is it that animals and sailors
are the only ones
to use the stars to help them
get to where they need to go?

DOES EVERYTHING
HAPPEN FOR A REASON?

Yes, because it has all happened before
so what we are witnessing is something
happening for the second time, or the
Third, or fourth etc and so on.
Now, the question is why?

We are part of multiple strings that act
on their own by trial and error.
This was designed that way so nothing
could interfere. Nothing.
Do the strings have a life of their own?
Yes, but only for trial and error purposes.
Once the trial and error becomes set where
no other trials are needed, then
God's plan become law,
And the strings vanish.
And we are okay with that.

DON'T UNDERSTAND

I don't understand Death.
I don't like it either.
If it is true that we go to Heaven
and live there forever,
why can't the middle step
be eliminated and just…….
well, never die?
What would be the cutoff?
Right now, it's Death.

EMAIL POLICE

I used to threaten friends for not
watching their e-mails by reporting `
them to the E-Mail Police.
Now with Facebook, Twitter and so on
E-Mail is almost forgotten and gone
the way of Faxes. Sad.
Threatening them with the E-Mail Police
never worked.
They just laughed.
What to do ? What to do?
I decided to try something new.
Now I talk to them face-to-face,
or call them on the telephone, and
sometimes I send them a hand-written letter.
You say that is not new?
Well, it's new to them.

EVIL TWIN

Everyone has an Evil Twin.
We all have done something
we are not too proud of
be it ordering many items we do not need
or eating something very sugary when
we are not hungry yet claiming we
are on some kind of diet.
When caught by others we simply
blame it on our Evil Twin.
Truth be told: they do not criticize
us too much because they know
they also have an Evil Twin

FREEZING A MOMENT

The father had his young daughter sit on the chair
In front of him.
He wanted to savor and freeze the moment forever,
although he knew that could never be.
The seconds, minutes and hours would take over.
He saw her in a pretty yellow dress, blonde
hair with pony tail, and smiling innocent,
and trusting eyes.
His eyes welled up.
"Why are you crying, Daddy?"
"Those are happy tears because you are the perfect
little girl I could ever hope for."
"Can I go and play now?"
"Sure, go ahead"
Years later that little girl had a little girl of her own,
and she placed her daughter in a chair before her,
and she understood what her father had done years ago.
She wanted the same thing, knowing it could never be.
Her eyes welled up.
"Why are you crying, Mommy?"

FIRST LOVES

We all have had them.
The first was Susan H. when I was 10.
I couldn't ever get close to her on that bus
from school going back to Pepperrell AB
In Newfoundland. So I worshiped this very
pretty girl from afar.
Next was Marion G., 6th grade at Travis
Elementary, Travis AFB, CA.
Very pretty too, and we won $.25 each for a best face
on a ice-cream cup. Never talked to her since, but
always looked her way.
Next was Carol T. in 7th grade. Very pretty, but
It didn't last long. I must have done something
that she didn't like and it was over. Bummer
Then there was Edna F. waiting for the doors
to open to go into High School.
To look at her I would have to catch my breath.
There she was in a light blue dress suit, pink shirt
and black paten leather shoes with the ever present
pony tail and a very pretty smiling face.
Took me 4-yrs to talk to her and we went on
a couple dates, then she went back to her previous
boyfriend. Bummer.
Hey, I memorized Shakespeare's 18 Sonnet for her.
Still know it.
Yes, we have all had them, seen and gone in the blink
of an eye. Seems that is what first loves
are all about.

GETTING TO HEAVEN

Here's the thing.
Looking back on everything
I don't see how anyone can
actually get to Heaven.
I mean it's just too hard.
Yet, I don't see how anyone can
end up in that other place either and
that place seems easy enough, but
when we were created as Humans
is that like saying there is no hope for us?
We are not all that bad to end up in
that other place, but
It does seem like an easier path.
Woe to us.
That's the thing.

GIVING A NAME FOR
A FOOD ORDER

We are often asked to give our name
for an order at a fast-food store.
I have decided on "Your Majesty"
In the past I have used:
"Your Highness"
" Sir Robert"
But "Your Majesty" seems to
work the best.
And yes,
we all have fun with it.
Try it....................

GOLF ANNOUNCERS

Most are very good, and
we enjoy them, but
when they tell us that the ball is
3-feet away from the hole and
we can see it's no more than 1-foot,
they lose credibility.
Oh, they say they are there and
can see better than we who have
to rely on TV distortion.
Really?
One more thing:
They tell us how difficult a shot is.
Okay, but they forget that most of us
play golf and can tell right away
If the shot is difficult.
As for me, the most difficult shot is
when I take a club out of the bag.
HA!

GOOD TIMES

Good friends of long ago
still creep into my memories
of good times we had.
Looking back I wish we still
were in touch.
Do they think the same?
Time and distance are the culprits,
that are blamed.
To make contact again may not be
a good idea
because everything changes and possibly
In dramatic fashion.
It is sad to say those good times were
mandatory but are never to be repeated,
and must only remain memories of our
good times.
Very sad.

HAPPY VS RESPECT

You often hear:
I just want you to be happy.
That's fine if Happiness lasts, but
it doesn't, and there comes a leveling off.
What should people say to those who
they want to be happy?
They should tell them to always
maintain Respect
for themselves and for others, and
in time Happy will take care of itself, and
there will be no leveling off with Respect
for themselves and for others.
However, truth be told:
I want you to be Happy.
Ha!

HELLO SUMMER

Hello Summer.
Yeah, we saw you hiding behind
the snow, ice, freezing rains and extreme cold
as I am sure you didn't want any part of that too.
Now we have a favor to ask:
Try not to be too hot, humid, without wind.
You could work on a cooling wind, that's okay;
And a gentle breeze at night would be almost perfect.
But we know you have your orders and won't listen to us.
Already our days are becoming shorter and we know,
in time, you will be looking for a place to hide again
as Cycles rule.
Yes, yes, Cycles rule. We know that.
However, in the meantime we are at your mercy.
It's still Summer.
Be nice.

HER EYES

The most important features
she carries with her
are her eyes
that tell me she cares
with one direction.
What do they look like?
I have no idea except
they are focused only on me.
What they look like are of
no consequence
because her gaze bores
into my soul and that
tells me all I need to know,
and that is to say her loving gaze
and I are truly one.

HOLIDAYS

I hate holidays (except for one),
4th of July.
My TV shows get pre-empted,
and there are TV shows that promote the holiday.
Some of my favorite stores are closed or their
hours are reduced.
No mail is delivered.
I think we can still have the holiday
without upsetting TV shows, Store hours,
and mail deliveries, but
will that happen?
No way.
In time there will be a holiday
for each successive day of the week
to be called Holiday Week with many more to come.
When that happens the country will stop
and be at the mercy of almost anyone with evil designs.
Of course, they don't think that way.
Get it?

IDEAS

So I had a lot of ideas,
But couldn't remember them later on.
And muttered, "What was I thinking."
I decided to write these ideas down.
And so I did.
Later on I took a look at what I had written.
I couldn't make out my own handwriting.
"What was I thinking?
Now what do I do?

IMMORTAL WORDS

Let me set the record straight:
I was the first one to use these words:
A new Beginning circa 1983.
Now everyone says it. Bummer!
Also, this expression:
Doing the best I can with what I have to work with.
Circa 1963.
Again, I hear it all the time.
Am I given any credit? Of course not.
What to do? What to do?
Yes, of course, there is a story behind 1983 and 1963
that produced those immortal words above.
I need to find out who is stalking my thoughts.
Anything you wish to share?

INACTION

I wonder where she is now,
and I keep thinking of her.
Back in the day, I saw her
many times but had no
chance to talk or even be
near her.
Of course, I regret never
doing anything,
She knows I did look her
way often and I wonder
what she made of that.
I wonder where she is now,
And does she ever think of me?
Probably not.
Inaction is worse than a crime.

INVISIBLE

I am invisible:

- Seen and not seen.
- Heard and not heard.
- `There and not there.
- Always alone even in a crowd.

She looks my way but doesn't see.
I look her way

TRULY INVISIBLE

It's something there and not there

- Seen and not seen
- Clear and not clear
- Heard and not heard
- In the mix and not
- Part of and not

It's true: some people are
truly Invisible.

JOBS IN HEAVEN

Should we get to Heaven
what would we do there?
We see and hear of people
going there and returning
telling us of all the friends
and relatives they met who
always seem to be available to greet the
newcomer.
Were they given time off from their
Jobs?
What are their jobs?
What would be our jobs should we
get there?
However, think for a moment.
Does it matter?
Really?

KNOWING

She said she didn't vote because she
had to work.
He told her she needed to keep up with
what is going on to keep kids in the know.
She said she knows that.
She didn't say because she has a boy, a girl
a 7-yr old, an 8-yr old or a kid.
She said: I know. I have a child.
When she used the word "child" he knew
everything about her that he could ever want to know.
That was pure love.

LIARS

Even when a known liar
tells the truth,
we know
he is still lying.

LIMBO

The period between Christmas and New Year's
is like Limbo.
One thing is over, and the next thing
hasn't happened yet.
What to do? What do do?
Decorations seem out of place, but
too soon for the new decorations.
What to do? What to do?
Limbo is a waiting room
remembering what was and thinking
about what is to come.
Somewhat exhausted people go to work
hoping to rest up for that new Day;
then after that another kind of Limbo sets in
until another Christmas and then
it starts all over again.
We only leave Limbo on Christmas Day and on New Year's Day.
After that we are back.

LOOSE ENDS

Most of my life I have had to clean up
loose ends.
I did think that I completed all that was to be
completed, but not so
as I was told by those who saw me not complete
all of what they asked.
Some companies still owe me money and that
is a loose end whereby I must write them a letter
and explain my case.
Is that a good loose end?
Not at all, and it will drag on, I am sure.
If I still owe them money, is that good loose end?
Yes, it is.
And I must comply sooner rather than later.

LOTTERIES AND CHAOS

It is often said there is no chaos in the Universe,
but there truly is when it comes to lotteries.
We need to understand that God may not be
saying NO.
He just might be saying NOT YET, and
we need to believe this
to keep
HOPE alive.

LOTTERY INTERVIEW

Whoever wins a big lottery
will be interviewed.
Suppose I won and was asked
"How does it feel to have won
a big lottery?"
My answer: " I feel as though
I just broke even."

LOTTERY TICKET

Some previous lottery winners
tell us they forgot they had a ticket
and when they remembered and checked it
they discovered they won.
Is that the key to winning?
For me the problem is this:
I never forget I have a ticket

LOVE

Yes, there are different kinds of love,
but there is one thing they all have in common:
a 100% protection factor.
When we love someone, truly love someone,
we want, above all, to protect that person
from everything that could cause even the slightest bit
of harm or discomfort.
If we could keep that person in our arms forever and ever,
that would be okay,
but that is not possible,
still it's a nice thought anyway.
Keep in mind that true personal love is this:
Each has each other as
the priority.

MAGIC 8 BALL

Remember those Magic 8 Balls
that used to answer every question we ever had?
Well, I thought they were gone too, but
someone I do not know sent me one and the answers
are nothing like we used to get.
For instance: I asked if I will ever win a lottery.
Ans: In your dreams.
See?
I asked if I will ever find love?
Ans: In your dreams.
What to do? What to do?
It's almost like there is someone alive in there
with an attitude.
That seems to be the only reply it has
as I did ask other questions.
I have an idea: I will ask if it knows
who sent this to me and if that fails:
does it know what a sledge hammer can do?
Stay tuned.

THE ONE THAT GOT AWAY

When I looked into her eyes
I saw everything.
When she looked into my eyes
she thought she could do better.
We tried but it didn't work.
She left and there I was with
an incredible memory of seeing
everything.
and that is all I have,
that memory.

MIRACLES

There are many miracles around today, but
we don't see them or rather, pay no
attention to them.
There are 2-miracles I would like to see now:
all blind people be able to see overnight;
and all children with any kind of illness be
cured overnight.
Wouldn't that be a very good step toward
World Peace?
However, if you still want to see miracles,
just open the door to the outside world.

MISSING THE DEPARTED

The old man sat
muttering to himself:
It's not right, they should all be here.
He was talking about all those friends and family
who had passed and he
missed them.
He rambled on: I know it's life and
It's ways, but it's just not right, and
I will never understand.

MOTIVATION

There is much that needs doing, but
I am too tired to do anything.
What to do ? What to do?
I have found the solution:
I bought a tool belt, and
put some tools in it, and
some may be needed,
some not.
Now things get done.
No time to rest.
Too much to do.
Why didn't I think of this before?
This actually works.

MY BOOK

M: So you read my book?

H: Yes.

M: What did you think of it?

H: It was okay.

M: Just okay?

H: Yes.

M: Did you ever write a book?

H: No.

M: if you did write a book, what would you say?

H: You said everything I wanted to say so why
     duplicate things.

M: Hmmmmm.........................

MY DAY OFF

M: My day off is on Saturday.

Q: What do you mean?
   You are retired. Every day is your day off.

M: Yes, in a way, but Saturdays are special.

Q: How so?

M: I don't go anywhere on Saturdays.
   I stay home.

Q: Why?

M: Because everyone else is out there on Saturdays
   on the roads going everywhere at the same time.
   It's just too crowded. During the week they are
   all going one way: to work at the same time, but
   not on Saturdays which is a mess all day. And don't
   get me started on the stores...............

Q: So what do you do on these Saturdays at home?

M: Wait for the rest of the weekdays.

Q: What about Sundays?

M: Actually, not so bad and I think most are resting
   up from all that going-here-and-there on Saturdays.

MY HEROES

Mickey Mantle, Roy Rogers, Gene Autry
Yes, there are more, but these are
the major ones.
Who can forget Mickey Mantle hitting
the longest home runs
Not me.
And Roy and Gene as Kings of all Cowboys?
Not me.
True champions all.
Gone?
Oh, no…………………..never.

MY LUCKY DAY

I decided to walk and not
ride up the hill with uncle
and friends.
I carried 3-metal rods each about
4-ft long and a sledgehammer to
replace boundary markers.
The Jeep went out of sight.
All was quiet, too quiet.
Then I saw a brown spot moving
up ahead. Could not see the head.
A deer, coyote or something else?
I ran down the hill still carrying all.
Kind of lost my direction until I saw
the blue plastic tarp the house-owner
covered something with.
Later the house owner said there were
reports of a coyote in the area.
Decided next time, if there was a next time,
that I would carry a shotgun with me to
Insure another Lucky Day.

NAMES

The mother said, "Do not call my son Mikey,
his name is Michael."
I said okay.
Everyone calls her daughter Elizabeth "Liz"
To date everyone calls Michael "Mike" or "Mikey"
I said "everyone."
Go figure.
Their father and I are the only ones to call Michael and
Elizabeth:
Michael and Elizabeth.
It's only right.

NICKNAMES

People often accuse me of giving nicknames
to various people.
Not true.
These people give themselves the nicknames
See Fred Astaire, who danced while
waiting for the subway at Union station.
He was pretty good too.
The guy who looked exactly like the Penguin
in a Batman movie. Very strange.
Lois and Clark, a married couple I saw in Church
and they truly fit the bill. Up, up and away............
If you ever saw them you would
agree with me.

NO POOPING IN HEAVEN

Most of us want to get to Heaven.
What we will experience there is
not clear.
We are told by religious leaders that
Heaven will be better than we have it here.
That's a relief since there are some things
that are annoying, and sometimes
troublesome here on Earth.
I believe it is safe to say there will be
No pooping in Heaven.
Pretty sure………………..

NO PROPHET

You have heard that no one is
a prophet in his own land.
Once you are known for something
you are that for the rest of your life.
Growth, maturity, balance
have no rightful place.
You are what you once were and
always will be.
Never to change.
However, once you leave that birth land
the world is different, and you only hope
those in the new land never
meet the ones in the old land.
And if they do meet
once again
you are not a Prophet.

ODE TO A COFFEE POT

You did good for these many years,
always right on time providing the
warmth always expected.
But now you've slowed down,
and coughing and sputtering
And taking a very long time.
Too long a time.
Something is wrong, and I don't
know how to fix you.
Then one day that I will never forget
you became silent and I mourned
for you.
Good-bye old friend.
I know I have to unplug to replace you
and put you away out of sight,
But I will keep the memory of
what you did for me those many years,
and tell others how you were good.
Good-bye old friend.........................

OTHER LIFE

Life does exist on other worlds, but
we are not to obtain proof of this
at this time,
But wait, what about all those
Structures, Drawings on rock, Caves, Pyramids above
and below the oceans........
Who built them?
Not humans without extraterrestrial help.
So we go along knowing these things are there,
but don't really believe Aliens helped.
Truth is most don't believe Aliens exist.
How foolish.
Just take another look at those Structures, Caves
Drawings and Pyramids all over the world to include those
below the oceans.
Yes, take another look.

PARKING

Ever notice that when you park
In a large grocery parking lot
no one is on your left or your right?
But when you come out of the store
There is at least one car on your left
or your right or on both sides.
You see many open spaces those cars
could have parked, but no
they are right beside you.
Why?
It's simple:
People don't think about you
or your car.

PAST LIVES

Did you ever go to bed
asking who you were the years
before you were born?
I do that from time to time, but
nothing ever comes of it.
Maybe we never had past lives?
No, I don't believe that as there
are a lot of evidences out there of people having
past lives.
And yet many do not believe this, but
I do.
Hey, I will keep asking the question and
who knows..........maybe I'll get an
Answer one day.
Hope I like it.

PASTEL SUNSET

I have a feeling that everything in Heaven
is of a pastel nature.
We are given glimpses of it when we see
a pastel sky sunset not knowing what we are seeing.
We look at it in awe and sometimes we feel
touched by it, but not knowing why.
Then we pass and go on about our lives.
But what if it were true, as I believe it is,
then what?
We see a softness of lights in an array of numerous colors,
almost transparent.
Almost.
There seems to be a beckoning to us
or am I reading too much into this?
Maybe.

PASTEL SKY

I could watch a pastel sky all day long
What a treat.
I do believe it is the beginning to where
Heaven is.
I want to instantly go there and become
One with it.
Not possible.
Now it's starting to rain
Gone is the pastel sky and dark clouds
now come.
I still have my memory of that pastel sky
and know it will come again to add to
my memories.
Can't wait.

PERFECTION

A friend says he was told he was not perfect.
Said he replied: How rude!
Says there he was thinking he was the be all and end all
of all things and to be told none of that is true.....
again he replied: how rude!
Asked What should he do?
Of course he tells everyone he is not perfect.
Says he lies a bit, but they go away happy
believing in something that isn't true,
never knowing how wrong they are.
Says telling all he is not perfect is the perfect thing to say.
Asks: Isn't this is what perfection is all about?
Says: Perfect.

PREQUELS

We are seeing many prequels.
Too many.
And for what reason?
Truth be told they who produce
have nothing new to give us, and
think we need to see everything
that happened before.
Now here is the better truth:
We don't.

PRIVACY

Inspired by Dave Schartung

Many people want privacy, but
they have Facebook, Twitter,
Instagram, and so on.
Want privacy?
Stop those above,
stay home,
don't go out much,
Keep the small circle of friends,
Don't get involved in anything.
The only law that guarantees privacy is:
there is no law to do that.
The solution:
become that island.

PUMPING UP MY FOOTBALL POOL

Inspired by Bob Cunningham

Today is 21 June and why do we care?
Because the days will becoming shorter.
And, why do we care?
Because we 're getting closer to Football season.
And why do we care?
Because we'll be playing soon.
That's why..........................

RASPBERRY COFFEE

I love everything raspberry
until I tried raspberry coffee.
Terrible stuff.
When I went to Jeff's TV
repair shop I poured myself
a cup of coffee,
and there was a hint of
raspberry coffee in there.
Jeff had tried raspberry coffee,
didn't like it, but forgot to
clean the pot.
Great minds tried something
at almost the same time and
agreed raspberry coffee was
terrible stuff.

REGRETS

This is what my friend told the
very young girl he had a thing for:
I have 3-Regrets and 1-promise.
I regret that I am not closer to your age.
I regret that you are not closer to my age.
I regret that we have never won a lottery,
but will keep trying.
I promise to never cause you any
discomfort or obligate you in any way.
Just be yourself.
He said he will get over this.
Now, we know he never will.
Really.

REMOTE VIEWING

The military uses
Remote Viewing to see
where the bad guys are and
what they are doing.
Can it work for me to find
the one I Iove?

RESOLUTION

Q: You know, God could end all this strife.

M: How so?

Q: Simply by showing up in the sky.

M: Like a Sighting?

Q: Yes.

M: Don't believe that is how it works.

Q: Well, it should. Why go thru all this?

M: Something about mysterious ways, I think.

Q: Do you think a Sighting might work?

M: Probably.

Q: Do you want to tell Him?

M: No.

REST

Sometimes nothing is going on
and it's a good time to rest.
However, others are not so restful
and keep coming around for me to
do things with them.
What they don't realize is that I am
still a novice down here and must
wait until my probationary period is over.
To go against that rule is disastrous and that
also includes my benefits are limited or -
In some cases – not at all.
If there was a way I could g et someone
above to help me
I would do it.
But then they would probably die of fright
and join me down here with no privileges
whatsoever.
Still, there must be a way……………………
I'll rest on it for now.

RESULTS

When things happen and the result
is not a good one, we ask:
Is this the way it is supposed to be?
Also when things go right, do we ask:
Is this the way it is supposed to be?
Probably not as we only ask this when
things go wrong.
The thinking is that something could have
been done to change a bad result.
Really?

RETIREMENT

Since I retired friends want me
to go here and there.
They think I have nothing to do,
and travel would be good for me.
Ha!
I am at a place where I do not have
to be anywhere, and no one tells
me that I have to be at a certain place
at a certain time as when I was working.
No, I like it this way and if I want to go
somewhere I go.
If truth be told and known,
I had more time to myself when
I was working.
Very busy and I just do not have the time
to go anywhere.
I like it this way.
Isn't that what retirement should be?

SAINTS

We have been told that when we get to Heaven
we become Saints.
But down here on Earth the only ones
who can become Saints, after death, are those in religious
arenas: Popes, Cardinals, Bishops, Priests,
Brothers, Sisters and Nuns.
I know - and I am sure you also know - some
who can and should be considered Saints
Hey, I am talking about more than "our Saintly mothers"
How do we get to make them Saints?
Any ideas?

SAME GIFTS

I am sure this doesn't happen too often,
but it does happen
when the same gifts are exchanged
at the same time.
Case in point:
Colored lights for a toilet bowl motion detector;
and rubber ice-trays.
I was involved in one and heard about the other
on the same Christmas day.
Great minds, eh?

SEEING GOD

If you want to see God,
you can.
Just look
into a child's eyes.

SMALL WORLD?

In Disneyland you will hear the song
"It's a small world, don't you know."
But in truth this Earth/World is very big.
Now, I am not talking about people connections.
Go travel and you will realize how
big this planet/world really is.
Why should you travel to realize this?
Because
it's not a small world, don't you know.

SMALLEST PYRAMID

I paid a lot of money to be able to
climb the smallest pyramid at Giza,
out of sight of all the tourists, of course.
Well, there I was standing in front of
the first boulder and it stood over my
head by a couple inches.
How in the world was I going to get
over the first rock?
I had no idea.
Everyone was looking and I jumped as
high as I could and was able to get
on top of the boulder leaning on my arms.
If I wasn't in shape playing tennis I don't
think I would have even thought about
climbing one of the Wonders of the World.
The boulders got smaller as I and my guide
made our away up.
You would be surprised at all the room
at the top.
Enough for 4-persons to sleep comfortably.
Of course, I took pictures, but
I do regret not having taken more.
Bummer.

SORBET

After lunch the waiter
asked if I wanted dessert.
I said yes, and he told me
they have a wonderful
Sorbet.
I had never heard that name
and had no idea what it was.
I didn't want him to know I
didn't know what Sorbet was.
What to do? What to do?
Finally, I said, "What flavors
do you have?"
He rattled off a list of flavors
and when he came to Lemon
I said, "Lemon."
You can never go wrong with Lemon.
The Sorbet came and I thought
to myself: it's just a refined
version of Sherbet.
Now I know what Sorbet is.
Quite good, too.

STUTTERING

I stuttered as a kid.
I employed all kinds of "tricks"
to not stutter.
Some worked, but not always.
In my 20s, I listened to a warehouseman
In the USAF who talked with a cadence
that almost sounded like singing.
When a stutterer sings, he/she doesn't
stutter.
I tried that warehouseman's cadence.
It's like saying Ahhh and then talking
over the Ahhhh. See?
I didn't stutter.
Over time I was able to speed up
my speech to a point it didn't sound
like a singing hum below the words
I used.

SUNDAY

Feels like a Sunday?
Why?
We see people going to church
and we don't recognize them
in their dressed up clothes.
Fewer cars on the roads.
Not sunny enough.
No kids outside playing.

SUPER HERO

Q: So you are a Super Hero?

S: Yes

Q: Can you fly?

S: No.

Q: Do bullets bounce off of you?

S: No.

Q: Do you have X-Ray vision?

S: No.

Q: Are you faster than a speeding bullet?

S: No.

Q: I am confused. What makes you say you are a Super Hero?

S: I always do the right thing.

Q: Always?

S: Always

Q: I think you may be on to something.

TABLOIDS

At the supermarket,
I watched a woman look intently
at the latest tabloids for many, many
celebrities.
She seemed somewhat confused
so I told her that what she sees on
the covers is all the news she will
need and that she won't find
any other news within.
Now she seemed satisfied.
My work was done.

TALENT

I believe most everyone has a talent
known or unknown.
Inklings of a talent should always be encouraged.
Once a talent is known life becomes better.
Yes, most need to explore many avenues to see if
a talent exists.
As for me you ask?
I'm still looking……….

TEAM FAMILY

When in the USAF we played
Baseball in a small town league
and everyone on this one team
had the same last name.
We played against a family, which
was somewhat unusual.
I pitched and sometimes would
call out to my team on the sidelines
"Who is up now?"
The reply was always the same last
name.
Making light of the moment I
called out, " What again!"
Yes, somewhat humorous but
they were very good players.
Who won the game?
I cannot honestly recall.

THAT PHONE RING

Before VCRs, my mother used to call me
right about 10-minutes before my one-hour
program was over.
I asked her not to call me at that time because
that is when all is revealed.
She did comply.
Now with VCRs, DVRs it doesn't matter much,
but my mother is no longer with us.
Now I look at the clock at 10-minutes before
the hour and wish the phone would ring
once more.

THE ANSWER: SIGHTING

The answer to a complete World Peace
is very simple.
We need a Sighting by those in Heaven,
but we have to convince them to stop
watching Star Trek TV shows that
talk too much about the Prime Directive.
Now just how do we do that?
That's the real problem.
How indeed?

THE ANSWERS?

1. Does God Exist? Ans: Yes.
2. When we die, what happens? Ans: Some go to Heaven, some do not.
3. When will the Earth end? Ans: In the year 3301
4. Is there life on other planets? Ans: Yes.
5. Will a big Asteroid destroy the Earth? Ans: No.
6. Will Aliens from another Planet contact us? Ans: they already have.
7. Will Aliens destroy us? Ans: no.
8. Are Aliens from other worlds friendly? Ans: Some are, some are not.
9. Will there ever be peace in the World? Ans: No.
10. Will Disease be eradicated? Ans: No, but lessened greatly.
11. Do Ghosts exist? Ans: Yes.
12. Will there be a WWIII? Ans: Yes.
13. Will the US win WWIII? Ans: God will be the only winner.
14. Why is the Sky Blue? Ans: It was designed that way.
15. Why are we here? Ans: To serve God.
16. Did we have past lives? Ans: Yes.
17. Why did we have Past Lives? Ans: To achieve Atonement.
18. Will I ever win a big lottery? Ans: No.
19. Should I stop playing the lottery? Ans: Yes, but you won't.

These Q&A came to me in a dream. Are the answers correct? I have no idea, but number 18 concerns me.

THE BALANCE BEAM

Recently, I watched the Olympics in Rio.
All was good, but there is one event
that needs to be cancelled out, terminated,
done away with.
The Balance Beam.
This is one of the most dangerous pieces of equipment
ever conjured up for a balancing event.
A miscalculation on a backward flip can ruin
a girl's life for good.
Years ago I wrote to the IOC and told them so.
Of course, I received no answer, but I think
their comments may have gone this way:

- And who are you?
- Why are you bothering us?
- You know better than us?
- If you don't like it, don't watch

And, of course, I don't and won't.

THE BEACH

When we were kids my aunt would
take us to a beach.
Sounds good, right?
However this beach was loaded with rocks
It was Ouch, Ouch, Ouch all day long.
Why were we at this beach?
Then her boyfriend showed up.
Ah.....................

THE DARK SIDE

Let's go to the Dark Side,
and see what that is all about.
Will it change my heart to allow
me to vow harm to all?
Would there be point to this?
What would I gain?
Let's say I did this and then
discovered I was now the only
one alive with no one else to harm,
But, perhaps, only myself.
So the question remains,
why go
to the Dark Side?

THE ECLIPSE

The Eclipse came and went
The birds didn't understand,
The horses and cows didn't care and kept
on grazing
The dogs and cats thought it was cool
and went t their food bowls, which
were nowhere to be found.
Humans sat and stared at the sky

THE EYES HAVE IT

When I look into a child's eyes
I think of puppies and kittens.
All three have so much in common.
They are joyful and bounce around
without a care in the world, curious,
hesitant, daring, and trusting …. sort of.
As an adult I am reminded that we were once
a part of this triangle of joy.
What happened to us?

EXPOSURE

I had a dream.
I think it was a dream
I was in a cemetery and my guide
walked me to a specific grave.
He said, this person was
the greatest violinist ever.
I said I never heard of him.
Was told that was because his parents
never exposed him to music, but had
they, then he would have been the
greatest violinist ever.
I had to ask: are there others like him?
Was told: yes, many, many. Very sad.
I had to ask: What about me?
Very sad. Your parents never exposed
you to anything as they were always
busy with jobs.
I had to ask: is it too late for me?
The dream ended.
Pretty sure it was just a dream......................

THE LAMBORGHINI

When I was a boy I had a chance
to sit in a Lamborghini.
It took me 10 Minutes to get in it,
and about 15 minutes to get out.
Afterwards I told my friends that if
they ever had an urge to rob a bank,
to never use a Lamborghini.

THE LAND

I used to tell my uncle that he never
enjoyed the land he owned as
he was always working on it, never really
sitting down enjoying all before him.
Of course, I was wrong.
I do enjoy this land that was his,
and wish I had more of the ambition
to work the land as he did, but
truth be told he enjoyed his land
the only way he knew how:
by working it day after day.
As for me I enjoy this land that was his,
now mine, as I sit and purview all before me
and wish he was here to do the things
he enjoyed most
as the land could use some work.

THE LOOK

I saw her only once
and she looked my way
for only a split second, but
In that time I saw the future,
without her, but her look
told me what could have been
had her gaze lasted a little longer

THE ONE THAT GOT AWAY

Many of us have that story
about the one that got away.
My story goes something like this:
When I looked into her eyes
I saw everything.
When she looked into my eyes
she thought she could do better.
We tried but it didn't work.
She left and there I was with
an incredible memory of seeing
everything.
and that is all I have,
that memory.

THE PAST

The older I get the more
I think of my past.
I recall friends I am no longer in touch with
and wonder if they recall me and the good times
we had.
It's somewhat depressing to know there were
good times, and now no more with them.
Newer friends now occupy the present and I will,
In time, call these days as "the good old days" once again.
How many "good old days" are we permitted?
It's a shame those days will all blend together and also
a bigger shame that everyone, I knew, does not
know everyone else.
The same can be said for them, of course.
It's a shame we all don't know each other and
I, for one, would like nothing else.
But the way of the world won't permit it as
we all do not go down the same roads.

THE PENNY

Lately, I have been having some very weird dreams,
And I will start to write them down after I tell you about this one.
There I was having talk with the Devil. Yes, that Devil.
Little nobody me has this dream with the Devil, that Devil.
He tells me to pick up a penny on the floor in front of me and
that all my wishes, desires and long life will be mine.
I just have to pick it up.
I say, "You mean I won't lose my Soul, do not have to kill anyone,
and not do bad things for all that to happen?"
"yes" is the reply.
Not sure what happened next, but as I waked away I looked
back and saw the penny still on the floor.
Slowly, I began to understand.
The Devil lies. Yes, that Devil.
If you see a penny on the floor and are told to pick it up:
Leave it.
Now to get to those other dreams……………..

THE RED HAIR GIRL

I never thought this would happen to me
I know Charlie Brown has his Red Hair Girl,
and now, it seems, I do too, but not really.
What a beauty.
Now what do I do?
I see her look.
I look and so far nothing.
I just cannot get her out of my head.
I know I am too old for one so young,
and she truly is.
I know what Albert Finch would say,
but I don't want to listen.
This is too intense for me.
Is she on my path and we must meet?
Stay tuned,
this isn't over.

THE ROADS NOT TRAVELED

I always wondered about those other roads
always by-passed because I had no business
going there.
This is about the physical roads, not about
those other ones.
So one day, I decided to go down those roads
to see if I was missing anything.
Nope.
Nothing new.
So if you wonder about those roads that you never
traveled down, take a lesson:
There is nothing to see, but
go down those roads anyway
to get them
out of your system.

THE VISIT

We are told that we will visit other
Spirits down here.
Yes, we are Spirits and have no
resemblance to what we looked like above.
We are told that many will be former
celebrities we knew about when we
were above, but we will only know
this should that Spirit tell us.
Most will not as they are tired of all that
celebrity, which is hard to believe.
Many will not be here as they have Ascended
or not.
However, down here we are told we are all
equal and no one Spirit is above any other.
Not sure why this visiting is needed
as no one spirit can do anything for another

THERAPY

I am in Therapy due to
a pulled muscle in my left leg.
Got it trying to get into
a very high step-up into a
big pick-up.
When I tell others I am I n
Therapy
They kind of laugh and think
it's a boon-doggle.
How wrong.
The Therapy exercises help
the healing process and I
am getting better all the time.
These friends will come to
know how the exercises help
when they find themselves
In Therapy.
But, truth be known, I hope
they never have to go
to Therapy.

THOSE ARTISTS WHO
HAVE PASSED

We remember songs and stories about artists who we
liked in life and who are now gone.
The question remains:
Who will take their places?
Yes, some will come and we will like
as those of Before,
but we feel there will never be the
quality of those as Before.
We imagine maybe they are in Heaven
doing their thing.
Yes, a kind of a silly thought,
but it's all we have
until we get there, too, and see for ourselves.

THOUGHTS AND THINGS

Am pretty sure you heard the expression
Thoughts are Things.
Well, they really are.
My thoughts follow me everywhere.
Yes, the bad ones.
I see them all the time.
They just won't go away.
The harder I try to get rid of them
and not see them, the worse it gets.
They are there in various disguises.
What to do? What to do?
Sometimes I can get the good thoughts
to push the bad ones out, but
this doesn't last long.
I don't consider myself a bad person
but these bad thoughts are not helping.
The real solution is to find that special girl
who is definitely on the Path, okay....
my Path.
Yes, I hear you when you say:
Good luck with that.

TIME

I am convinced there is no such thing as Time.
All there is, is Motion.
Everything is in Motion going somewhere,
Including this Planet and the Galaxy.
Even those seemingly at rest
are, in fact, in Motion.
When one Motion begins and ends
we mistakenly call the interval in between: Time.
Wrong.
But truth be told there is no beginning to Motion
as it is always there,
always moving, and there is no ending or stopping it
But the real question is:
Where are we going?

TO RHYME OR NOT

Q: You write Poems?

M: Sometimes.

Q: Do they rhyme?

M: Mostly no.

Q: Poem should rhyme.

M: They don't have to.

Q: Yes, they have to.

M: No, it's the thought that counts

Q: Like when you give a lesser gift when
a more expensive one was anticipated?

M: It's not like that.

Q: Do you try to rhyme?

M: Sometimes, but it doesn't always work out.

Q: Why not?

M: Sometimes the thought gets lost when
there is a concentration on a rhyme and
the rhyming word really doesn't fit.

Q: And that justifies a non-rhyme?

M: Again, it's the thought that counts]

Q: Poems should rhyme.

M: They don't have to.

TRUE LOVE

I met an elderly man who said he has been
married for 62 happy years.
I asked him:
When you look at her now, do you
see her as you first saw her then or
as she looks now?
Smiling, he replied:
Both

TRUE WORDS

I wrote a book and it was published
to my surprise.
I read the thoughts in poem form as though
they were someone else's words
and asked myself
Do these words ring true?
And I answered: yes.
To some that will sound pompous, but
I was totally honest with myself.
All of you can do the same thing.
I am awaiting your book.

UNIQUE

No doubt about it.
I am unique.
Just like everyone else

VOTING

She said she didn't vote because she
had to work.
He told her she needed to keep up with
what is going on to keep kids in the know.
She said she knows that.
She didn't say because she has a boy, a girl
a 7-yr old, an 8-yr old or a kid.
She said: I know. I have a child.
When she used the word "child" he knew
everything about her that he could ever want to know.
That was pure love.

WAITING DAY AFTER DAY

There was a man who sat all day long
day after day, after day, after day.
They asked him why he sat
day after day.
He said he was waiting.
Waiting for what they wanted to know.
He replied: contractors

WAITING

Q: What are you doing?

P: Nothing, just waiting.

Q: For what?

P: The other shoe to drop.

Q: What are you talking about?
       I thought things were going good for you.

P: They are, too much so……………

Q: ……..and you think something will happen?

P: It always does.

Q: Something big?

P: Doesn't matter big or small.
       It will happen. It always does…………..

Q: And the other shoe……..?

P: Will drop. Yes.

Q: What will you do when it does?

P: Deal with it ……… as always.

WAS IT A DREAM OR SOMETHING ELSE?

Walking down the street one day in the city
I saw my uncle on the other side.
I stopped to look at him and noticed
he was wearing his farm work clothes
and not his priest clothes with white collar.
He stopped and looked at me, too, but said
nothing, not even an inkling that he knew me.
He looked at me for a time as did I with him.
Then he walked away as did I.
My uncle died in 2007.
Did I dream this or was this an actual sighting?
Thinking on this for some time I decided he
looked at me as though I had passed on and
he wasn't sure what he was seeing,
and the same with me.
I still cannot figure out if this was a dream or
did it actually happen in real life as this came
to me as a memory.
A memory? From what?
Did I get a glimpse into another reality?
Did my uncle?

WE WILL BEAT YOUR ASS

Bob and Bill were talking football,
NFL football.
Bill wanted to know if his team would
play Bob's team this year.
Bob said, "if we do, "WE WILL BEAT YOUR ASS."
Both laughed.
It was a funny thing to say.
Both found out that their teams did NOT
play each other this year.
Upon leaving Bob said, " If we did play you
this year, WE WOULD BEAT YOUR ASS."
Again both laughed as
that was funny too.
Maybe you had to be there....................

WEEKDAYS

Every day of the week has its own behavior
and we know it to be true.
For instance, a day will seem like a Monday
because of the weather and what we normally
do on a Monday.
The same applies to all other days of the week.
The problem arises when we do Monday things
and someone tells us, "It's Thursday."
Ooops!

WHAT TO CALL IT?

Hmmm…………what to call it this time?
Poems of Sorts 2
Poems of Sorts Plus
Poems of Sorts Plus Other Stuff
Snippets
Snippets and Other Stuff
Poem Snippets and Other Stuff
More Ammo for Stand -Ups
Thoughts in Poem format
Another Mixed Bag of Thoughts
It Comes To This
Nobody Cares (but me)

WHEN WILL I DIE?

In the 1990s I responded to a test
which results will tell me when
I would die.
I was asked if I smoked, how much;
If I drank, how much;
If I ate a lot of junk food, sweets etc
And there were other questions, too.
All asking: How much? How much?
The results: when I am 79.
Now here's the thing:
I don't do any of those things anymore.
Should I take another test ?
I have decided not to do that because
I do not want to know.
79?
Really?
We'll see.....................

WHO'S IN HEAVEN?

Had a dream where I was in Heaven.
So I asked around for a few friends.
I was told Mike was not here.
"What do you mean he's not here.
Of course he is, check again."
Came back, still not here.
"That can't be. Why is he not here?"
Was told: Can't say,
but maybe because of this, or that
or even because of this or that.
I go to see Mike and ask, "Do you know
what this or that is?
I tell Mike he better know what
this or that is and go take care of it.
Then the dream ended.
Now do I tell Mike about the dream?

WRITING

I only write about things I know.
I only write about things I know are good
and because I know they are good.

YANKEE DUGOUT

Had a dream whereby Casey Stengel
bought the old Yankee dugout.
It made sense and we were pleased
to know the dugout will still be used
to house all the stars long gone from us.
We could forever imagine these stars
talking among themselves appreciating
each other and their feats.
Oh, the stories they would tell
as Casey watched sometimes
also seeing himself
among these greats.
It was a very nice dream.

YOU KNOW YOU
ARE OLD WHEN

you are addressed as "Sir" or " Ma'am"

IN THE GRAVE

WATCHING

I lay in this pew of a grave,
And watch and listen
to all above
noting
no one watches me anymore,
but only think of me as once upon a time,
having done nothing of note, nothing to quote,
nothing ever done, hardly any fun.
What would they say if I suddenly appeared?
But I laugh to myself as this cannot be done.
Still a fun thought nevertheless I cannot hide.
But now I need someone to turn me on my side
and watch and listen from that view
until I need to be turned again within this pew.

ORIENTATION

We must attend orientation
to learn the dos and don't
while here.
We are told there will be
a ton of rules:
can't do this, can't do that
Oh, and we cannot speak
as that is reserved for when
probation is over with.
Just like above one cannot
fight City Hall here, too.
But it may not be too bad,
But what if we did get out of line,
what would they do to us?
Kill us?
Ha!
Good one.

COLD IN THE GRAVE

Well, winter is almost upon us
and I wonder if I will be okay
with the Cold.
This last summer was really hot.
I'd say I almost died if......................
I need to talk to the Caretaker
to see he will get me a winter home
In the summer,
And a summer home
in the winter.
By the way where was he this summer?
Hmmm.......something strange going on.
It seems I will have to get close
to this Caretaker.
This isn't over.

STILL HERE

Still here.
Doesn't look like I'll be going anywhere soon.
Hard to know what will happen next as
the Caretaker doesn't say much.
Yes, we have a Caretaker, but am not sure why.
He's never around when you need him.
Where does he go?
In the meantime I watch things above and
have learned I am becoming a distant memory.
When above I was a faint memory, not a distant one.
Maybe that's a good thing.
We have a meeting later this week and
I'll ask if there is anything new and good
That someone above has said above me.
You have no idea how important that is to us..
This is our ticket to hmmmmm............not sure where but
It's better than down here I am told.
Can't be late for that meeting.

ROAMING

No, we cannot go anywhere we want.
We can roam all around the Yard
(we call this the Yard)
There is a rumor going around that
some have gone beyond the Yard, but
most of us are content to just watch
everyone above and see how they are
doing with our not being there.
We can see a mistake about to be made
and can do nothing about it.
Sad, I know.
Need to check out that rumor of those
who say they can leave at Will.
It would b e fun to leave the Yard and
scare the living daylights of someone
about to make a mistake.
Hope that rumor is true.

OTHER PATHS

There's a rumor going around
that says we can find out what
would have happened to us had
we chose those other paths we did
not choose in life.
How cool it that?
Problem: we have to wait until our
probation over and that's when we
leave our bones and become spirits.
Why is this so? No idea.
Those other paths will take some time
we are told, but hey,
we are not going anywhere;
we died. Remember?
Stay tuned....................

REST

Sometimes nothing is going on
and it's a good time to rest.
However, others are not so restful
and keep coming around for me to
do things with them.
What they don't realize is that I am
still a novice down here and must
wait until my probation is over.
To go against that rule is disastrous and
that also includes my benefits are
limited - or in some cases – not at all.
If there was a way I could get
someone above to help me,
I would do it.
But then they would probably die of fright
and join me down here with no
privileges whatsoever.
Still, there must be a way..................
I'll rest on it for now.

MOVEMENT

We move the way a spirit moves,
otherwise our bones or clothing would present
a problem and probably get caught on something.
We can go anywhere in the yard and later
we are told we can go to other places, providing
we are good.
There are a lot of rules down here, and
are stuck here until the time comes when
we Ascend to another place,
hopefully where many of our friends and family
think we already are.
"Bless their Souls"

CELEBS

One would think that now
we have the chance to meet
Celebrities we knew about in life.
But no, that cannot happen as
they are in another section we
are not privy to.
Bummer.
Some say there is a possibility
that we could meet some Celebs
when we get to the final
destination.
Not sure what that means.

FRIGHT

Now that probation is over
I can join the new singing group
that will go above in the yard.
Of course, none of us can carry a tune,
but to do it in the presence of a couple
on a picnic nearby a deceased relative
will really be cool, especially when we
get that relative to sing a few bars badly,
of course.
But to see the fright of those on a picnic
is worth all the gigs we get from the Caretaker
who warned us not to do that.
Yeah, right, Gigs!
No, they cannot see us, but hear us: oh yes.
Wish I had a camera to see those faces
when I need a lift.
And you didn't think we had any joy down here.
Hey, we still have out memories.
Wonder how many Gigs we will get?

MORE GIGS

Now I am on another probation
with others.
Am told I have more Gigs coming.
Told I am not in the running for
roaming the oceans.
I need to ask the Caretaker if he did
anything against the rules when
he first came down here
so he should understand.
Why is he still here?
He should have ascended long ago.
We had another meeting and he told
us that he was told he could ascend, but
he is more valuable here for the time being.
Time? What time?
Time means nothing to us.
Roaming the oceans would have been nice.

NOTHING GOING ON

So here I am with nothing to do;
Roaming the oceans is out;
Nothing else going on.
Might as well be.............
Wait a minute........I am
Bummer

SOCIALIZING

Getting to know anyone down here
Is not easy.
They don't want to socialize and
are more concerned when they will
Ascend.
Can't blame them, I suppose.
As for me I can do many things
that I couldn't do above.
Okay some of it is not exactly legal
and if caught all they can do to me
Is extend my stay here and tell me
I will never Ascend.
My plan is to somehow go above
and scare the living daylights out of
someone who owed me money and never
paid me.
I have to do that so no one knows I am above.
Now, how can I do that?
I need to find a friend who will cover for me
and if that person is caught it must
be someone who
Is not afraid of more Gigs.
Need to plan this carefully.

A GUIDE

I don't know who is reading this,
but all I am trying to do is give
a heads-up to let others know
what is going on down here to
make this very new experience
a little more familiar when someone
makes this trip.
Call it a Guide if you want.
There is so much more that
no one above really knows about.
Maybe that's a good thing, but
I feel some knowledge is a helpful thing.
I cannot describe anything that happens
when we Ascend as that is a mystery
even to us down here.
All I can really say is that there is life
down here, but not like anything you know
up there.
Stay tuned, there's more to come.

PAGES

Some wonder how I get these
pages to someone above.
When I first heard that this
was possible, I could hardly
believe it.
But here we are.
How is it done?
There is a room that only
a select few can go into.
It's supposed to be for showing remorse,
or gratitude and it's completely private,
but if the Caretaker ever found
out I am not doing it for remorse or
gratitude,
I would lose many privileges,
but this all happens by talking about
anything we want and by magic
or something, the pages appear
above.
How was I able to get into this room?
It's complicated and I cannot say,
as I fear the Caretaker has Ears
everywhere.

ABOUT THE AUTHOR

I know, I know this is what was in Poems of Sorts. I never change. Bob is a transplanted New Yorker who now lives in Virginia. He has a BS in Business Management from Concord College, Athens, West Virginia. He served four years in the USAF, worked overseas in Saudi Arabia for 9.5 years, and later recruited for overseas military contracts. He writes poems that rhyme or not and still writes movie reviews, but not horror movies - so he can sleep at night - for friends who need to know what their children can watch and he puts those reviews on IMDb.com.

CPSIA information can be obtained
at www.ICGtesting.com
Printed in the USA
BVHW042125100220
572014BV00011B/114

9 781643 676265